Junior Library of Money

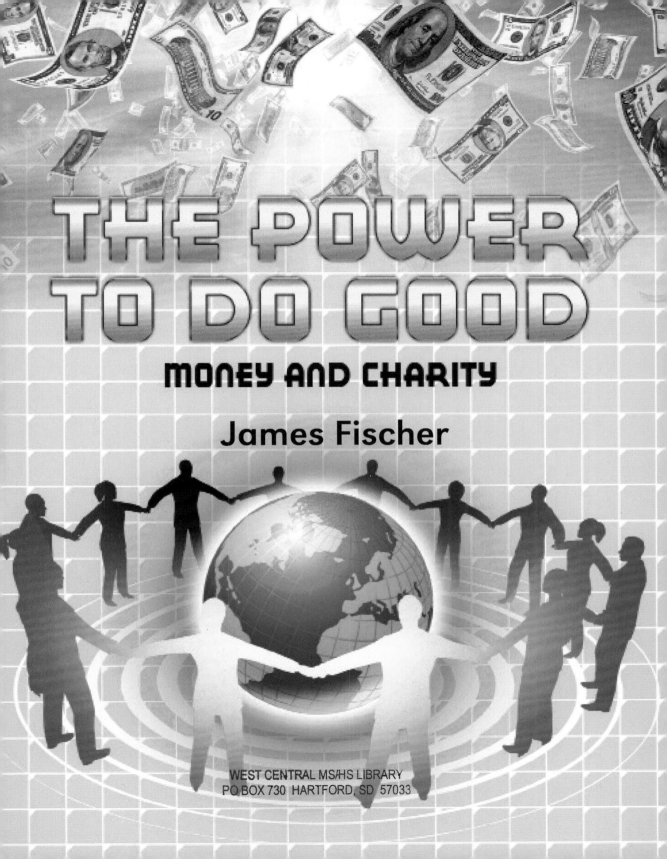

THE POWER TO DO GOOD

MONEY AND CHARITY

James Fischer

MASON CREST PUBLISHERS INC.
370 Reed Road
Broomall, Pennsylvania 19008
(866)MCP-BOOK (toll free)
www.masoncrest.com

First Printing
9 8 7 6 5 4 3 2 1

Library of Congress Cataloging-in-Publication Data

Fischer, James, 1988–
 The power to do good : money and charity / by James Fischer.
    p. cm.
 Includes bibliographical references and index.
 ISBN 978-1-4222-1769-6 (hbk.)   ISBN 978-1-4222-1759-7 (series)
 ISBN 978-1-4222-1888-4 (pbk.)   ISBN 978-1-4222-1878-5 (series pbk.)
 1. Charities—Finance—Juvenile literature. 2. Nonprofit organizations—Finance—Juvenile literature. I. Title.
 HV40.F537 2011
 361.7—dc22
                    2010028432

Design by Wendy Arakawa.
Produced by Harding House Publishing Service, Inc.
www.hardinghousepages.com
Cover design by Torque Advertising and Design.
Printed by Bang Printing.

Content$

Introduction

Our lives interact with the global financial system on an almost daily basis: we take money out of an ATM machine, we use a credit card to go shopping at the mall, we write a check to pay the rent, we apply for a loan to buy a new car, we set something aside in a savings account, we hear on the evening news whether the stock market went up or down. These interactions are not just frequent, they are consequential. Deciding whether to attend college, buying a house, or saving enough for retirement, are decisions with large financial implications for almost every household. Even small decisions like using a debit or a credit card become large when made repeatedly over time.

And yet, many people do not understand how to make good financial decisions. They do not understand how inflation works or why it matters. They do not understand the long-run costs of using consumer credit. They do not understand how to assess whether attending college makes sense, or whether or how much money they should borrow to do so. They do not understand the many different ways there are to save and invest their money and which investments make the most sense for them. And because they do not understand, they make mistakes. They run up balances they cannot afford to repay on their credit card. They drop out of high school and end up unemployed or trying to make ends meet on a minimum wage job, or they borrow so much to pay for college that they are drowning in debt when they graduate. They don't save enough. They pay high interests rates and fees when lower cost options are available. They don't buy insurance to protect themselves from financial risks. They find themselves declaring bankruptcy, with their homes in foreclosure.

We can do better. We must do better. In an increasingly sophisticated financial world, everyone needs a basic knowledge of our financial system. The books in this series provide just such a foundation. The series has individual books devoted specifically to the financial decisions most relevant to children: work, school, and spending money. Other books in the series introduce students to the key institutions of our financial system: money, banks, the stock market, the Federal Reserve, the FDIC. Collectively they teach basic financial concepts: inflation, interest rates, compounding, risk vs. reward, credit ratings, stock ownership, capitalism. They explain how basic financial transactions work: how to write a check, how to balance a checking account, what it means to borrow money. And they provide a brief history of our financial system, tracing how we got where we are today.

There are benefits to all of us of having today's children more financially literate. First, if we can help the students of today start making wise financial choices when they are young, they can hopefully avoid the financial mishaps that have been so much in the news of late. Second, as the financial crisis of 2007–2010 has shown, poor individual financial choices can sometimes have implications for the health of the overall financial system, something that affects everyone. Finally, the financial system is an important part of our overall economy. The students of today are the business and political leaders of tomorrow. We need financially literate citizens to choose the leaders who will guide our economy through the inevitable changes that lie ahead.

Brigitte Madrian, Ph.D.
Aetna Professor of Public Policy and
Corporate Management
Harvard Kennedy School

♥Sharing

Sharing is something our parents tell us to do when we're really little. We learn the Golden Rule—do unto others as you would have done unto you—as it applies to our toys, our books, and our food. But sharing isn't just for little kids. It's a lifelong lesson that makes a lot of sense even as we get older.

Charity is one kind of sharing. Donating things that you have a lot of with people that are less fortunate is an important way to share what you have with others. It's a sort of indirect sharing, since you usually have to go through a middleman. You usually can't just hand out donations to people in need. Instead, **charities** and **nonprofit** organizations are what let you share your **resources** with the rest of the world.

What Are Your Resources?

Resources are things we use to accomplish goals. You might be familiar with natural resources, like water, oil, and metal, which people use to make manufactured products. Every human being also has personal resources, which they can use to fulfill their own goals. Some of the resources you have as an individual are money, time, special skills, and material goods.

Some people have enough resources to succeed in life, but others don't. This might be because their home was destroyed in an earthquake, they were born into poverty, or they fell ill and had to pay hospital fees. Whatever the case, the fact remains that some people have plenty of resources and others don't have enough.

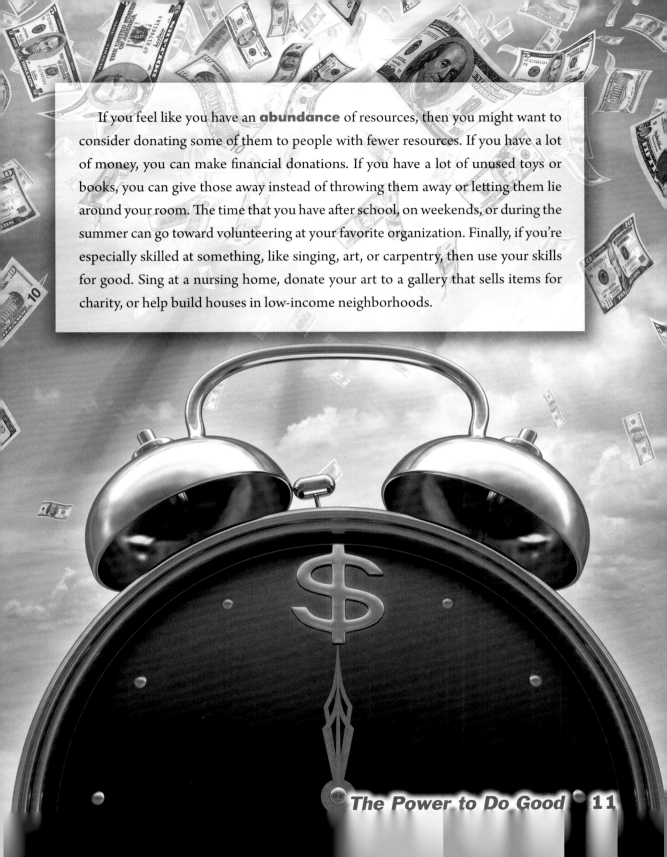

If you feel like you have an **abundance** of resources, then you might want to consider donating some of them to people with fewer resources. If you have a lot of money, you can make financial donations. If you have a lot of unused toys or books, you can give those away instead of throwing them away or letting them lie around your room. The time that you have after school, on weekends, or during the summer can go toward volunteering at your favorite organization. Finally, if you're especially skilled at something, like singing, art, or carpentry, then use your skills for good. Sing at a nursing home, donate your art to a gallery that sells items for charity, or help build houses in low-income neighborhoods.

WHAT CAN YOU AFFORD?

As a kid or young adult, you probably don't have a lot of extra money of your own. How much money can you really afford to donate to charities?

There's no set amount of money you should give away to charities. It depends on how much money you have in your savings account, if you have a part-time job, what you're saving money for, and how strongly you feel about making donations. But you can probably make more donations than you think. Look around your room. There's likely to be lots of things in your closet or under the bed that you don't need or want, and didn't even realize you still had. Giving that stuff away is a donation, just the same as giving away money. You can definitely afford that!

Don't rule out donating some money, though. Many charities only accept money donations, so if you really support a specific cause, then consider showing your support with money. Small amounts are perfectly okay. Unless you have an steady income, or have large amounts of savings, then don't feel obliged to donate really large amounts. After all, if you don't have that many resources, then it's hard to give them away to other people.

Starting to give to charities now will make donating a habit when you're older and have more money. Once you realize that it helps people and makes you happy, then you'll make it a lifelong practice. If you feel strongly about donating, then you can always donate larger amounts after you start earning more.

WHY SHOULD YOU?

Why should you give to charities? After all, you're not getting anything in return. You might think you're cheating yourself if you donate $20 of your own savings to a charity instead of buying something you really want. It's your money, so why should you give it to someone else who didn't earn it?

There are actually lots of great reasons to donate your resources to others. It's the right thing to do to help others in need. If you needed a place to sleep for the night, then you'd probably want someone to help you out and find you a bed. It's the same thing in reverse: you're helping others. We're all human, and we all need help from time to time. It's only right to use your own resources, if you have more than enough of them, to help other people.

Giving to charities leaves you with a warm feeling inside. It usually makes us happy to know that we've helped people out. Scientific studies have shown that donations do make the **donor** happier! Also, knowing that you have enough money or other things to donate makes you realize how good your own life is, and gives you a sense of pride to know that you own enough resources to have a comfortable existence.

Donating also teaches you that money and material goods aren't the most important things in the world. Once you part with a little bit of money or some old clothes, you might realize how much more helping people is worth than just the amount of money you're donating or however much the clothes are worth. You have to add on the value of connecting with and helping other people. Can you really put a price on making a difference in the world?

What's Important to You?

Figuring out where to donate can be harder than you think. There are thousands of charities out there and picking just one or two might be overwhelming.

You can start one of two ways. First, you can think about what you're interested in and what social issue is most important to you. Then you can do research on charities that promote that cause. Or, second, you can take a look at the charities in your community and pick one that you think does important work.

The first option requires you to sit down and consider what you're worried about in the world. Examples of social issues where you could donate include poverty, hunger, homelessness, environmental destruction, health care, and animal welfare. You probably know more about some of these issues than others, or feel more strongly about one than the rest. That's okay—it's pretty hard to fight poverty, cancer, and animal cruelty all at the same time! Deciding on one or two causes to donate to is the right way to go, as long as you're helping someone.

Take a look around you. What do you care most about? If you love your pets, then maybe you want to think about donating your time or money to an animal shelter. Or if your grandma battled cancer a few years ago, then maybe a cancer research fund is the right choice for you.

For each social issue that inspires you, there are many different charities. To pick just one or two, search around on the Internet. Try out a site like GreatNonprofits, and search by categories of issues. Maybe one will jump out at you.

Keep your eyes peeled for charities where you can donate. Some of the larger nonprofit organizations get mentioned on the news (on television, in the newspapers, in magazines, or on the Internet). If you want to donate your money to natural-disaster victims, for example, then pay attention to news stories about natural disasters, which often reference the charities that are helping out at the scene of the disaster.

If you choose this route, then your money could end up going to large national or international charities. If you'd rather keep your donation closer to home, in your own hometown, then you'll have to do some different research. In that case, it will be easier to look up what charities are active in your community, and then decide which issue you care about most. If you live in a city, then there will be all sorts of charities to give to, but if you live in a smaller town, your choices might be a bit more limited.

Look in your local newspaper, pay attention to the local news, and ask your parents and friends for suggestions for local charities that might need your help. If you're lucky, then your town has a database or website devoted to listing all its active charities. If not, be more creative and keep your eyes open. Often, some charities will set up donation collection bins in local supermarkets or malls. They hold televised fundraisers, especially during the holiday season, and sometimes run telemarketing drives to ask for money over the phone. All these things point to the names of charities that are active in your community, and that might be worthy of your money or time.

Ways to Give Your Time

DID YOU KNOW?

Choose to donate your time to a variety of places. Soup kitchens are run by churches and hunger charities, to provide meals to homeless and hungry people. They always need volunteers to help serve the food. Homeless shelters also need people to help.

Sometimes sending money away to a good charity just doesn't make you feel like you're helping anyone, if you can't see what effect your donation has on other people's lives. You'd rather be more involved in what the charity does, and to see what your money is used for. Lots of people would

Hos-
pitals
are great
places to volun-
teer. You might work
at the gift shop, visit with
patients, or file and retrieve
medical documents. Animal shelters

DID YOU KNOW?

are volunteer options for people
who enjoy working with
animals. Work often
includes playing
with the ani-
mals.

rather actively help at the charity of their choice, so that they can see the difference their donation makes in the world.

Your time is just as valuable as your money. Consider volunteering, which is another way to say that you're donating your time. You'll get to see how a charity is run, what it does, and how it uses other people's donations of money or material goods. You'll get to meet other people with the same interests and **passions** as you, and best of all, you'll get to see just how your charity—and your time—is making a difference in your community.

More Ways to Give Your Time

Vol-unteer-ing at nursing homes involves spending time with older people, serving them food, reading them stories, or just talking.

DID YOU KNOW?

If you're interested in helping people with disabilities, check out the Special Olympics games all over the country.

What if you don't want to volunteer on your own? If you're nervous to start volunteering at a charity you don't know anything about, then volunteering through your youth group or school could be a way to break into the volunteer community comfortably.

There are lots of ways you can donate your time through organizations with which you're already involved. Religious centers often organize volunteers on certain days, or have regular volunteer programs they've set up with charities in the local community.

Your school probably also has some sort of volunteer program. There might be a teacher who organizes volunteer trips, or a club that is dedicated to volunteer activities. Ask your guidance office or your favorite teacher if they know of volunteer activities through your school.

Environmental charities work to improve the environment, cleaning up trash, protecting wildlife, and promoting good environmental behavior.

DID YOU KNOW?

Also consider volunteering with the Red Cross, where you can help with disaster relief or blood drives.

THINGS YOU CAN GIVE AWAY TO OTHERS

Your money and time are two of your resources that you can donate for the good of others. Here's a list of some other things you can give away:

- Clothes from your closet that you haven't worn in a year or two
- Books you've already read and don't want to keep
- Old electronics, like mp3 players, laptops, and cell phones
- Old eyeglasses that you've replaced with new prescriptions
- Bikes you've outgrown
- Toys you're not interested in playing with anymore
- Furniture you don't want

Donating your old things to people who really need them is a great idea. Rather than throwing them away, or letting them lie on your floor, find a place to donate them instead. If you don't need that old cell phone you replaced a couple months ago, and someone else does, then why not give it away to a charity? You'll have cleaned up your room and helped others at the same time!

Where Can You Give Your Things?

Donate old clothes, furniture, toys, and household goods to your local Salvation Army or Goodwill Store, places that specialize in selling second-hand goods. Old books can go to your local library, which probably has periodic book sales.

Some charities have collection bins around the community. Hunger organizations often put bins for canned food in grocery stores, eye doctors might have bins for used eyeglasses, and electronic stores sometimes have bins for used cell phones. Around Christmas-time, the organization Toys for Tots puts out bins for used toys. The charity then gives the toys to children in need around the country.

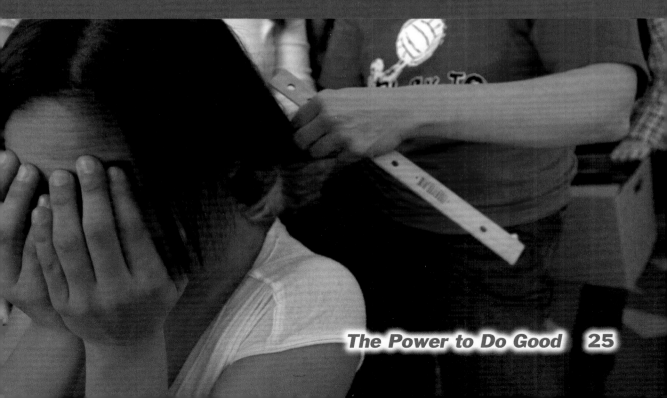

Places to Give Your Money

Money is still a great gift to donate, even if you have also decided to give away your clothes and volunteer your time. When you give money to charities, you give them the power to decide how to use it. Since you don't work at a particular charity, you probably don't know what sorts of things it needs to buy to help the most. For example, if you give an animal shelter money, employees or volunteers can choose to buy food,

DID YOU KNOW?

A quick list of places to donate money to include food pantries, homeless shelters, animal shelters, the Red Cross, hospitals, conservation groups, medical research programs, and large nonprofits like Habitat for Humanity or Heifer International.

vaccinations, or cat toys, depending on what is most needed right then.

Once you've decided to donate money, and have chosen a charity, you have to figure out how to do it! Many of the larger charities have online forms you can use to donate over the Internet, if you have a credit or debit card. If not, most places accept a check or cash amount through the mail. Find out the address of your charity of choice and send along your donation. Addresses will be listed online or in the local yellow pages.

More Ways to Give Your Money

Fundaisers are one of the easiest ways to donate your money. You run in to all sorts of fundraisers without even searching for them: bake sales at craft fairs and car washes on the side of the road are two pretty common sights. If you already have a charity in mind where you'd like to donate, check the website or give them a call to find out when they're having their next fundraiser. It might be a plant sale or a booth at a festival. Whatever it is, make a point of seeking it out, so that you can hand your money directly to a volunteer or employee of the charity.

The National Wildlife Federation (www.nwf.org) is a non-profit organization that is involved with protecting nature and wildlife.

DID YOU KNOW?

The American Red Cross (www.redcross.org) helps out around the world after a disaster. These are both good places to give!

Your school or religious center might also be a link between you and a charity. Religious centers often collect money from their members for a specific cause, and will then donate a large sum to a charitable organization. Schools and school clubs do much the same.

Donations also make thoughtful gifts. Several charities allow you to make donations in someone else's name, as a holiday or birthday gift. Your mom and dad would probably appreciate a small donation to their favorite charity in their name, as much as, or more so, than a new tie or pair of slippers. Donation gifts let recipients know you care about them, and have put time into a meaningful present.

However you choose to give, you'll know you've touched others's lives. Children in schools around the world, people who are suffering after a natural disaster, and even the Earth's wildlife, all need your help in one way or another.

Saving to Give

Donating money takes a little bit of effort on your part. Before you ever give anything to a charity, you need to figure out how much you want to give, and how much you can actually afford to give.

Don't let your finances limit you. You might not have enough money right now to give as much as you want, but you can always save some to donate later. There's no harm in waiting a few weeks or months before you put your donation plan into action. In fact, it's pretty admirable.

Say your goal is to donate $50 to a charity that fights poverty. You only have $30 to spend right now, and you're not sure you want to give it all away to charity. You also earn $5 a week in allowance. How do you reach your goal?

Start by setting aside some of the $30, say half. There's no reason you have to give away all your money, but as long as you save some for charity, you're heading toward your goal of $50. Then put every other week's allowance into your charity fund. You'll have $50 in about three months. If you want to donate sooner than that, then you'll have to save more every week.

Even if you're really dedicated to donating money to the perfect charity, you might still be tempted to spend it on yourself instead. A good plan of action is to keep the money you're saving in a safe place. Keep it out of sight in a piggy bank in your room, so that you can keep track of your money and remind yourself that you want to give to charity. Put all your extra change in there, and you'll have $20 or more before you know it.

An even safer place to guard your charity money until you donate it is a bank account. If you don't already have one, ask your parents to help you set up a savings account. You can add money to your account as you get it, and you won't be tempted to spend it on the movies or on a new set of clothes if it's completely out of sight and out of immediate reach. Plus, while your money is in a bank account, it can earn interest. Every month, you get a little bit more money, just for having some money in your bank account in the first place.

Once you donate, you'll feel pretty good. It's always worthwhile to give money to charities, but you can feel that you're making a difference if you give larger sums all at once. Giving a charity $5 every month is just as helpful as giving them $60 a year, but there's just something **grati-fying** about handing over a bigger amount of money!

ways to
raise money
to give away

So you've got an even bigger goal. You're not satisfied with donating personal money, and you want to actually raise some more money to give away. That's a noble goal, and one that will take some planning. Some ideas you should consider are:

- Walk-a-thons
- Craft fairs
- Bake sales
- Car washes
- Garage sales
- Raffles

Get some other dedicated people to help out and start planning. The more help you get, the better organized you'll be, and the more money you can hand over to charity.

Be sure to advertise what you're raising money for. People who don't necessarily want their car washed will still bring it in for cleaning if they know that the money is going to a worthy cause, not into your own pocket.

Tailor your fundraiser to the time of year. Is it summer? Do something outside that'll get people's attention and get them to donate to your cause. Or if it's around holiday time, have a bake sale or craft fair to entice people to buy presents for their loved ones, while they help their community with their donations.

Wise Giving

Wait! Before you give your money away to just any charity, make sure you're donatining wisely. When there's money concerned, it pays to be extra careful.

While most charities are perfectly safe and reputable, a very few are scams set up to get people's money and run. You don't want to donate to these types of organizations, especially not when you could be donating to real charities that put your money to good use.

There are a few rules to guide you in making the right decisions about donations. First, find out if the charity is legitimate. If it's registered with the government, and seems to be organized, then you can probably feel safe giving it your donations.

Don't be enticed by appeals to your emotions, either. Images of starving children on TV, or pictures of sad puppies in cages at the animal shelter's table tug at your heart-strings, but they might not tell the whole story. As much as you might want to help these causes, do your research before you give in to emotional appeals. All social issues are equally deserving of your money, so be sure you donate to the one you want to help the most, not the one with the most emotional advertising campaign! You'll feel better about donating once you know that you're giving to an organization that really will help starving children and sad puppies, not one that funnels your money into private pockets.

Another tip is to find out where your money goes. Once your money leaves your hands and lands on the charity's doorstep, how is it used? This is a valid question, and any legitimate charity shouldn't mind that you're asking. Don't be frustrated if a charity can't tell you exactly what happens to your money specifically, since it probably gets lots of donations and doesn't keep track of what happens to every single dollar. However, someone should be able to tell you what the charity does with donations in general. If the person you're talking to doesn't have a clue, or can't connect you with someone who does know, then you might have a problem. Do some more research before giving that charity a donation again.

Having a clear understanding of where your money goes also makes donating more rewarding. Your money doesn't just enter some sort of pot and disappear; it actually helps somebody, somewhere! If you can connect your donation to an actual action taken by the charity, that makes giving much more rewarding. For example, if a charity shows you a picture of a house it built for a family in need of a home, you know that donations like yours made that house a reality. If you're just sending a check off through the mail, you can easily lose track of the fact that you're having an impact on the world. Proof of that impact makes donating more special, and might convince you to keep on giving.

Reputable Charities

A charity is reputable if it uses donations in the best way possible, to improve the world as much as possible. Reputable charities are well-organized, and have made a positive impact on the community.

Unfortunately, not all charities are as compassionate as they seem to be. Most charities are wonderful organizations that truly care about the cause they support—but a few are not. Occasionally, you'll run across a charity that either doesn't spend its money well, or doesn't even spend it on what it's supposed to.

There are two reasons not to give to a charity that you think is suspicious. First, the charity you're considering could spend most of its money on administrative costs or on advertising, rather than on the cause that it's supposed to be supporting. Second, the charity could be a front for an organization that steals money. It pretends to collect money from concerned citizens, but uses it to pay the people who run the "charity" instead.

Sometimes charities are well-meaning, but they are just not that organized. Then they might fall into the first category. Charities should spend significant portions of their donations on programs that they put in action to further their cause, whether that's medical research, food for the hungry, or after-school activities. They should spend much less money on advertising, fundraising, and running the office. If a charity is new, then it might need some time to get off the ground and start using its money efficiently. If you're donating to a brand-new charity, then use your best judgement to decide whether your money will be spent wastefully, or if it will help the charity get up and running and start helping your community.

There are a few types of charities that fall into the second category, organizations that steal your money. Be wary of small organizations that crop up to help disaster victims and of charities asking for money over the phone or via email. After a disaster like an earthquake or tsunami, some individuals take advantage of people's compassion and set up false charities to collect donations. Instead of giving the money to the disaster victims, they keep it for themselves. Some phone and email charities are also more likely to just take your money without giving it to the cause they claim to represent. Always ask to see something in the mail.

The vast majority of charities are honest, helpful organizations, but you should double check before you decide to contribute to any nonprofit organization. Taking a few minutes to check now will keep you from wasting your money on a charity that won't actually improve the world. Find out if a charity you're interested in donating to is registered with the government. If it is, then chances are that it's pretty safe to donate to it. The charity you're interested in should have $501(c)(3)$ status. This means that it is a government-recognized, tax-exempt nonprofit. It's not proof that it's a great charity, but it does mean that you can probably trust it not to take your money and run. If a charity has $501(c)(3)$ status, then it should display it somewhere on their webpage, brochures, or storefront.

Fake charities can be pretty tricky. They often have names that are very similar to real charities, to trick you into giving to an organization you think you trust.

DID YOU KNOW?

For example, the American Cancer Society is a real charity, but the National Cancer Association, is fake.

Researching Charities

Fortunately, there are ways to avoid charities that won't use your donations well. Researching charities is fairly easy, once you know where to look. First, check out Charity Navigator, a website devoted to reporting on charities. Charity Navigator routinely comes out with lists of top ten charities, including the ten highest rated and the ten lowest rated. You can search by specific organizations to find out their expenses, how much money they make in a year, and what they do with that money. The site also gives each charity a rating. It's a handy, quick tool to use to start your research.

A second step is to check with the Better Business Bureau before you donate. The BBB is an organization that monitors business and charities to make sure they're running honestly. It records any complaints that have been made about the charity, so that people like you can do their research. Check them out on their website, or find the local branch of the BBB near you.

If you're planning on giving to a local charity, ask around to see if anyone you know has already donated to it. Ask friends, family, teachers, or coaches if they've ever heard anything about your charity of choice, or if they've ever given any money to it. Chances are, if it's a big enough organization, someone you know will have at least heard of it, and can give you a report.

If it turns out that you find some problems with the charity you were going to donate to, then think about finding a different place for your donation. Look around for similar organizations that tackle the same problems, so that you don't have to start from scratch all over again when deciding where to donate.

DESIGNATE YOUR DONATION

Charities usually know best how to use the money they receive in donations. People who work at charities are very familiar with the social issues they're working with, and understand exactly how the organization is run. If everyone who donated told them exactly what they wanted them to do with their money, there would probably be too much money for some projects and not enough for others. Who wants to donate money to buy office supplies at an animal shelter when they could donate money to buy kittens and puppies new toys?

However, if you have a cause that's near and dear to your heart, and you want to donate money specifically for that cause, then let your charity know. Since you're the one giving money, it's fair to have a say in how it's used. It can't hurt to ask, since the most a charity can do is deny your request.

You can personally ask that your donation be used a specific way, but a more certain approach is to designate your monetary gift. If you donate online, there might be a check box somewhere on the page so that you can check off how you want the charity to spend your donation. If you're mailing in a check, then you could write a note in the memo section of the check, to let the charity know what to do with it.

Another option is to donate something other than money. By donating food, for instance, to a soup kitchen, then you know exactly what your donation is going to be used for. Giving material goods to a charity lets you determine how you help, rather than giving the charity the choice in how to use your donation. This might be the way to go if you'd rather have a little more control over your gift. It might make giving more rewarding if you can imagine the food being eaten, rather than just picturing the money you handed over in an envelope.

Make sure that whatever material good you're donating is actually needed. Even if you think donating something is a good idea, the charity might not really need that item. Maybe that food pantry needs pasta and bread to give out, but you gave them canned goods—and their shelves are already overflowing with cans. Check with the charity before you give them anything. The people who run it will appreciate your donation no matter what it is, but they'll appreciate it even more if it's something they need desperately!

BEWARE
of Telemarketers!

It's a familiar situation: the phone rings during dinner, and your mom gets up to answer. Someone on the other line starts in on a rapid monologue asking for money to support heart disease research. What should your family do?

Sometimes, you or your family will get a phone call from someone claiming to be from a charity asking for money. Maybe they are actually representing a legitimate charity, but maybe they aren't. You never know with telemarketers.

If someone asks you for money over the phone, never give it to them, even if it sounds like a worthy cause. Be particularly suspicious if the telemarketer asks for your or your parents' credit card number. This is extremely dangerous, and can lead to identity theft and stolen money. If the telemarketer presses you to give money or your credit card number, then you can be pretty sure he or she isn't really working for a reputable charity, and just wants your money.

If the telemarketer really is from the charity she's claiming to be from, and if that charity really is reputable, then she won't mind you asking for information through the mail. Simply ask if they can mail you a brochure, since you're uncomfortable donating over the phone. Meanwhile, if it sounds like a cause you want to donate to, you can do some research and find out more about this organization. You might find that it's a perfectly legitimate charity, and can feel comfortable giving them your money. When the brochure comes in the mail, you can feel good about sending in a donation.

What Are the Benefits of Giving?

Donating is the right thing to do, but that's not always enough **incentive** to do it. Keep in mind that there are also lots of personal benefits to giving money, time, or other items to charities.

Giving clothes, furniture, and other unused things lying around your house is a good way to clean out clutter. If you're like most people, you groan at the idea of cleaning out your closet or under your bed. You might be more motivated, though, if your goal is to give your old things to charity. Suddenly, those old sweaters and toys aren't just junk in your room; they're items that other people need. Once you get rid of all that old stuff, you'll have more room, and you can focus on the things that you own that you really care about.

Donating your resources just makes you feel good. That's about one of the best reasons to give to charities. Helping other people in the community makes humans feel good about themselves. Communities can be hometowns, states, countries, or even the globe. Donating money halfway across the world can make you feel more connected to the rest of the human population, which makes a lot of people happier. Research suggests that donating and volunteering not only make people happy, but it even improves health in the long run! The same research also points out that people who care more about money than about family, friends, or helping others are generally less happy. Giving away money shifts your focus from finances to relationships. It might even change your attitude toward life, making you see how important other people are compared to money.

Another benefit to giving is that it highlights how fortunate you are. You can afford to give away your things, whether that's money or something else. Not everyone is able to do that, so consider yourself lucky that you can be the one that's in the position of helping other people out.

Sometimes giving to charity can even help you get over the loss of a loved one. Most charities let you make a monetary donation in the name of someone else. Saying goodbye to people is hard, but if you donate to their favorite charity, then it might help you let them go a little bit easier. You'll know that someone else is better off because of your gift. You can also make donations to honor people who are still living. To say thank you to someone for helping you out, make a donation to a charity to help others.

Reflect on what giving to charity means to you. It's likely that you'll experience some or all of these benefits, but if you don't take the time to realize it, then you're not getting all the benefits that donation can bring you. Do you feel better about yourself? Have you thought less about money lately? Charity donations can be pretty powerful if you let them.

TAXES *and* Charity

One of the best reasons to give to charities, in a **monetary** sense, is because it's good for your finances. Most of the money you give to charity can be deducted from your taxes. You might not care about that now, since you probably don't pay taxes yet, but you'll definitely care someday.

The value of everything that you donated during a year—money, clothes, books, furniture, etc.—contributes to how much money you can take off from the taxes you owe for that year. As long as you keep an accurate record of how much you donated, you can state the amount and pay less in taxes.

Donating to charities because you get to pay less in taxes can sound pretty selfish. Most of the time, though, people don't act for purely **altruistic** purposes. It's part of human nature to act in ways that make ourselves feel good. Tax deductions are just a way to direct that selfishness toward a good purpose. You're still making the decision to help other people by donating, so even if you do get the extra bonus of a tax deduction, you're still acting on your impulse to make the world a better place.

Keeping Records

It's always a good idea to keep records of your financial matters, donations included. Keeping records makes you more conscious of how you're spending your money, and if you someday wonder where all your money went, you can just turn to your records to figure it out. In the worst-case scenario, if you find out that the charity you gave to was a fraud, then you have proof of your donation if you need it. It's also helpful to get into the habit of keeping records now, so that you don't have to learn once you're older when it's even more important that you know how to keep financial records because of taxes.

Start off by keeping a notebook that records your donations. Write down how much you gave, who you gave it to, and when you donated. You should also estimate the value of any items like electronics or clothes that you donate, and write that number down too.

Beyond that, there are a few things you should also try to do. If you can, get a receipt from the charities where you give. Receipts should have the name of the organization, the amount you donated, and when and where you donated. Don't worry about getting receipts for putting some coins into the Salvation Army bucket during the holidays, but if you make larger donations, especially in the mail or online, get something that officially says how much you gave. Also keep copies of checks, if you ever donated money by sending a check to a charity.

You should definitely get a receipt and keep it in a safe place if you've donated hundreds or thousands of dollars. After you hold a fundraiser like a bake sale or a walk-a-thon, you might find yourself with lots of money to give. That's a lot of responsibility on your hands, so make sure you get some sort of written confirmation from the charity that they've received your gift. You wouldn't want the check to get lost in the mail, or find out that it was for the wrong amount.

Why Give?

There's no federal law that you have to give to charities, and there's no punishment if you don't. So why should you give at all? Besides all of the benefits that you've already learned about, there are lots of answers to this question.

Something inside you probably tells you that it's just the right thing to do. All people depend on each other to live, whether that means depending on farmers to grow our food, companies to manufacture our cell phones, or teachers to help us learn and be successful. We're all connected to each other, even if we live on opposite sides of the Earth. Helping and giving to charity is one way to fulfill the obligations we have to all those other people with whom we're connected.

Another way to look at it is in terms of relgion and morals. Many of the world's religions teach that charity is a necessary part of being human. According to Muslim, Christian, and Jewish teachings, members of those religions must give a certain percentage of their income to the poor. Charity has an important place in Hinduism and Buddhism as well.

Even if you don't have a religion, you have a set of morals that tell you what's right and what's wrong. Helping make the world a better place through charity fits squarely into something that is positive and right.

Keeping Your Commitments

No matter how good your intentions are when you decide to donate, there's always the distinct possibility that you won't follow through. You might forget, spend all your money, or just **procrastinate** and never get around to it. However, it's important to keep your commitment to your charity of choice, once you've decided to donate.

Make donating a priority rather than something you'll do only if there's enough money left in your wallet and if you happen to remember. Your decision is important, so don't push it off to one side as something you'd like to do someday. If you want to do it someday, why not now? Be realistic. Start by donating a dollar or two, or giving away old toys or clothes, which you probably can afford.

Actually budget your planned donations into your finances. Plan ahead to donate to a charity or two, and you'll be more likely to do it. At the beginning of the month, decide how much you want to give away. Add that amount to the amount of money you know you need to spend that month on necessities. Subtract that total from the amount of money you have to spend that month overall, and you'll know how much you have to spend on extra things you want. If you don't include your planned donations in your budget, you very well could spend all your extra money on computer games and iTune downloads before you even realize it!

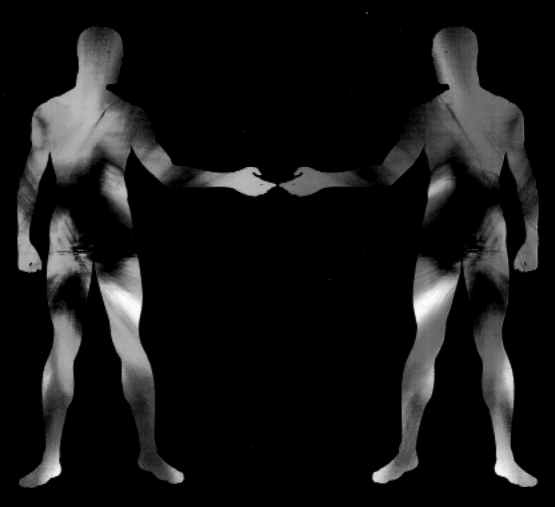

Change the World!

Can you really change the world by donating? It depends on what you mean by change the world. You probably won't singlehandedly solve poverty or rescue all the abandoned animals on Earth—but you WILL contribute toward small, positive changes.

Small steps add up. Your money could help feed a child for a week, or buy a box of nails to build a house for someone who was homeless. Your old clothes might keep someone warm during winter and your old books could teach someone how to read a little bit better. Finally, your time could make a nursing home resident smile or convince a family to adopt a dog. Don't doubt that your donations have made some sort of difference somewhere!

You're just one person, and by doing these things, you can change the world for the better in small ways. Now imagine that everyone you know

also spent some of their time volunteering or gave a monthly donation to a charity of their choice. That would make even more difference. Next, picture everyone on Earth who is capable of giving away some of their resources helping others by donating. That would make the most difference possible. If that happened, humans really could solve the problem of poverty!

One of the best things you can do is to convince other people to give to charity. Set an example for your friends: invite them to come with you when you volunteer, and talk to them about how great it makes you feel to give a small gift of money. If your family sees how excited it makes you, then they might decide to give too. Start a club in your school that's focused on volunteering and raising money through fundraisers. The more people you get to donate with you, the more difference you'll make—and the more positive changes you'll bring to the world!

Here's What You Need to Remember

- Everyone can afford to donate something, whether it's money, volunteer time, or used goods. Consider donating old clothes, toys, books, and electronics to those who need them most.

- Helping others, including giving donations to charities, makes people happy. In general, people who focus on relationships and giving tend to be happier than those who focus on money and financial success.

- There are thousands of different charities you can donate to. They work in your own hometown and around the world, tackling tough problems. The first step in giving to charity is to choose one or two organizations that match your interests and work with issues you're passionate about.

- Find a charity that's worthy of your money. Research some charities you're interested in donating to so that you know they'll handle your money well and make a difference in the world.

- Giving to charity makes you feel good about yourself, and helps change the world! Even the smallest donations contribute to solving problems like poverty, hunger, environmental damage, and animal welfare.

Words You Need to Know

abundance: Plenty, wealth.

administrative: Relating to the use or organization of a business, government, or other body.

altruistic: Regard or care for the well-being of others.

charities: Organizations that are concerned with helping the poor or needy.

donor: Someone who gives their time, resources, or money to help others.

gratifiying: Giving pleasure or satisfaction.

incentive: Something that has the ability to make doing something more appealing. For example, getting a piece of candy can be an incentive for doing your chores.

legitimate: Being used for the right purposes, in line with required rules or laws.

manufactured: To make something from raw materials into a finished product using machinery.

material: Actual, physical things.

monetary: Having to do with money.

nonprofit: An organization that doesn't receive any money for itself, but instead gives money to others for various charitable purposes.

passions: The things you are deeply excited about.

procrastinate: To put something off or leave it until the last minute.

reputable: Respectable, well-thought of.

resources: Something that can lead to wealth or production of a manufactured good; money, oil, natural gas, corn, and wool can all be examples of resources.

tax-exempt: Not required to pay taxes.

FURTHER READING

"Donating to Charity: A Guide." The Urban Institute and Indiana University, 2004.

Mutz, John and Katherine Murray. *Fundraising for Dummies*. Foster City, Calif.: IDG Books Worldwide, Inc., 2000.

Smith, Wendy. *Give a Little: How Your Small Donations Can Transform Our World*. New York: Hyperion, 2009.

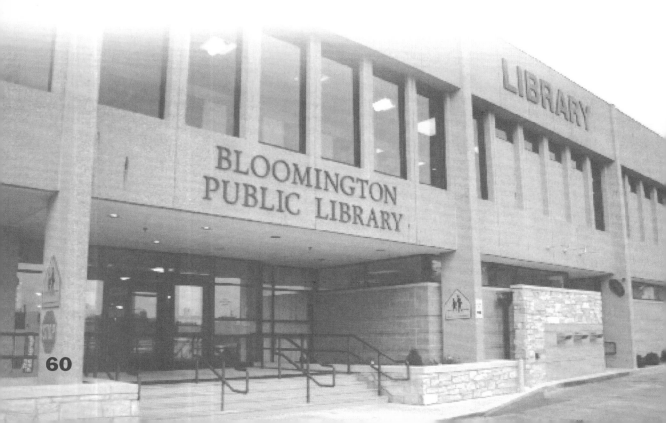

FIND OUT MORE ON THE INTERNET

American Red Cross
www.redcross.org

Better Business Bureau
www.bbb.org

Charity Navigator
www.charitynavigator.org

Fundraiser Insight
www.fundraiserinsight.org/ideas

IRS Search for Charities
www.irs.gov/charities/article/0,,id=96136,00.html

Locks of Love
www.locksoflove.org

The websites listed on this page were active at the time of publication. The publisher is not responsible for websites that have changed their address or discontinued operation since the date of publication. The publisher will review and update the websites upon each reprint.

Index

Picture Credits

About the Author and Consultant

James Fischer received his master's in education from the State University of New York, and went on to teach life skills to middle school students with learning disabilities. Money management and financial skills were a major part of his emphasis in the classroom. He has applied these skills to his writing for this series.

Brigitte Madrian is Professor of Public Policy and Corporate Management in the Aetna Chair at Harvard University's Kennedy School of Government. She has also been on the faculty at the Wharton School and the University of Chicago. She is also a Research Associate at the National Bureau of Economic Research and coeditor of the *Journal of Human Resources*. She is the first-place recipient of the National Academy of Social Insurance Dissertation Prize and the TIAA-CREF Paul A. Samuelson Award for Scholarly Research on Life-long Financial Security.